CU00651498

To:

_____

From:

_____

XO,
God

Other Books by Chris Shea

So This Is How Being a Grandmother Feels
Where Joy Begins
What Can I Give You?

"God is with thee."
Genesis 21:22

X O,
God

Chris Shea

Andrews McMeel
Publishing

Kansas City • Sydney • London

"God is with thee."
Genesis 21:22

XO,
God

Have you ever tried counting all the people you love?

xo God

1
2
3 4
5 6 7 . . .

"If we love one another
God dwelleth in us."
1 John 4:12

How about starting
today with a prayer?

Love,
God

" The whole earth is at
rest, and is quiet. "
Isaiah 14:7

Anyone you can
send a blessing to
today?

Love, God

"Behold, I have received
commandment to bless."

Numbers 23:20

Oh, just in case
you wonder who you
really take after....
        xo God.

Beautiful,
Good,
intelligent

"And God said,
    'Let us make man in
      our image.'"
    Genesis 1:26

I want you to
know how glad I
am   I made a y-o-u!
love,
God

"And God saw everything
that he had made, and,
behold, it was very good."
Genesis 1:31

Maybe someone at work (or at home!) will need an extra smile today!

XO God

"Do good."
Psalms 37:27

Gray skies make you
appreciate blue
skies, don't they?

Love, God

"A pleasant thing it is for
the eyes to behold
the sun."
Ecclesiastes 11:7

I love to see your
heart is content!
xo G.

"Godliness with
contentment is great gain".

1 Timothy 6:6

I can help you love even your enemies. Love, God

she started it!!

"Create in me a clean heart, O God."

Psalms 51:10

Gardening, like
life, requires much
patience!
                    love, God

 Told you
          you'd bloom!

finally!

"By little and little."

Exodus 23:30

Maybe take a
moment to reflect
on your riches today?

xo God

family
friends
health
kids
pets

"The blessing of the Lord,
it maketh rich."

Proverbs 10:22

Remember, often it
is better to be kind
than right...

Love,
God

You're
right
no you are!
No! You are
right!!

"He that covereth a
transgression
seeketh love."
Proverbs 17:9

Remember, I will always watch over you!

Love, God

All ways
and
always

"O Lord,
thou preservest
man and beast."
Psalms 36:6

I think LOVE
should be the
theme for the
day!
Love, God

"Love is of God."
1 John 4:7

If you ever want to
get even with someone,
remember this:
　　　Love, God

Thank
You!

"When a man's ways please
the Lord, he maketh even
his enemies to be at peace
with him." Proverbs 16:7

Take some time
for yourself for
healing, quiet, and
rest!   XO God

zzz

"Be still, and know
that I am God."
Psalms 46:10

Wonder just how
much attention I pay
to the details of your
life? Love, God

✦ - one!

"The very hairs of your
head are all numbered."
Matthew 10:30

Uncertain about
what steps to take?
xo God

"Follow me."
Matthew 8:22

Don't let anyone
steal your joy
today!
Love,
God

"Stand fast in the Lord."
Philippians 4:1

I wish you
Love in everything
you do today!
                    xo x g.

"Whatsoever thy hand
   findeth to do, do it with
      thy might."
Ecclesiastes 9:10

Feel free to take
some time to lean
on me...
Love,
God.

"The Lord is my shepherd;
I shall not want."
Psalms 23:1

Feel like ducking
out of sight for an
hour? Love,
    God

" Thou art my hiding place"
      Psalms 32:7

I like the idea
of a neighborhood,
especially when
family is far away...
Love, God

"Better is a neighbour
that is near."
Proverbs 27:10

Don't forget your
gratitude today!
XO God.

"Continue in prayer, and
watch in the same with
thanksgiving."
Colossians 4:2

Speak only loving
words today!

Love, G.

"Set a watch, O Lord,
before my mouth."
Psalms 141:3

What loving things
could you do in
secret today?
xo
God

"A good man out of the
good treasure of the heart
bringeth forth good things."

Matthew 12:35

Trying to
Kick a bad habit?
Love, God

"Behold, God
is mine helper."
Psalms 54:4

I hope you'll
have a really good day!
Love, g.

"For the Lord taketh
pleasure in his people."
Psalms 149:4

No matter what
may go wrong in
your busy life...

Y.O God

"He hath blessed;
and I cannot reverse it."
Numbers 23:20

While you work
around the house, I
am there, too!

XX O G.

"The Lord is round
about his people."
Psalms 125:2

I love seeing my
children happy when
they awake!
                    xo God

I love morning!

"Joy cometh
   in the morning."
   Psalms 30:5

Remember today:
How blessed you are!!

xx
God

"My cup runneth over."
Psalms 23:5

Think you could
share your riches
today? Tomorrow?
love, God

"The work of righteousness
shall be peace."
Isaiah 32:17

Isn't it amazing how
good you feel being
good to others?
Love, God

"The merciful man
doeth good to his own soul."
Proverbs 11:17

I love that my
children know I
am there for
them! *Love, God*

I can
help you
move that!

"The Lord will give
strength unto his people."
Psalms 29:11

How about counting
your blessings all day
today?   xo God

P.S. You'll be astounded!
P.P.S. Start small...

"Clean hands."
Psalms 24:4

I think friends were
a good idea, don't you?
Love,
God

" A friend loveth
at all times."
Proverbs 17:17

Only you could
make a peanut butter
and jelly sandwich
special!   XO y.

"He that is of a merry
heart hath a continual
feast."
Proverbs 15:15

Remember, you
never have to follow
the crowd!
Love, G.

"Be ye therefore
followers of God."
Ephesians 5:1

I will never lead
you anywhere you
can't find Me.

XXO God

"For I the Lord thy God
will hold thy right hand."
Isaiah 41:13

You know, they say
you can't steer a bicycle
that's standing still...

Love, gy.

"This is the way."

Isaiah 30:21

Speak Kindly today!

xo

God

"Let your speech be always with grace."

Colossians 4:6

I'm always close
in tense times!

Love,

God

" Truly my soul
    waiteth upon God."
        Psalms 62:1

When you search
for Me with all your
heart,
here's what happens!
xo
G

" I will be found of you."
Jeremiah 29:14

Goodness, joy, hope,
kindness. Share these
today!
　　　　Love,
　　　　　God

"Surely goodness
and mercy shall
follow me."
　　Psalms 23:6

If only you could
see that beauty
that surrounds you
from my perspective!
                X.o.G.

MY
VIEW:
Earth's
Beauty
PHOTOS

"The Lord looketh
from heaven."
Psalms 33:13

Don't hesitate to
share the blessing of
kind words today!

X O God

" The lips of the
righteous feed many."
Proverbs 10:21

although you may
be just a number at
the hardware store...

Love, God

NOW
SERVING
NUMBER

"I know thee by name."
Exodus 33:17

Say something kind
to a stranger today!

XO God

Nice
shirt!

Gee, thanks!

"Pleasant words are
as an honeycomb."

Proverbs 16:24

Facing a tough choice today? Trust yourself!!

xo G.

shall I pick this??

"The integrity of the upright shall guide them." Proverbs 11:3

You forgive someone,
they forgive someone else,
I forgive you. Kind of
a circle of love!!

XO g.

As do I

I forgive you!

"For great is thy
mercy toward me."
Psalms 86:13

Often I just can't take my eyes off you!

xo God

"I have loved thee with an everlasting love."

Jeremiah 31:3

Andrews McMeel Publishing, LLC
an Andrews McMeel Universal company
1130 Walnut Street, Kansas City, Missouri 64106

www.andrewsmcmeel.com

14 15 16 17 18 SDB 10 9 8 7 6 5 4 3 2 1

ISBN: 978-1-4494-6330-4

Library of Congress Control Number: 2014941960

ATTENTION: SCHOOLS AND BUSINESSES
Andrews McMeel books are available at quantity discounts with
bulk purchase for educational, business, or sales promotional use.
For information, please e-mail the Andrews McMeel Publishing
Special Sales Department: specialsales@amuniversal.com.